Study Guide for Decoding Hamlet

With Typical Questions and Answers

Steven Smith

Sherwood Press

CONTENTS

How to Use This Guide

This analysis of Hamlet intends to offer a study guide to readers who need a more in-depth view of the story.

This book is divided into questions, so the answers appear in a short essay style and may include repeated information. The questions are typical of what a high school student may experience.

I want to think all important questions have been either directly or indirectly answered. However, if you, the reader, feel something is missing, please reach out to me, and I will add it!

Happy studying!
Steven Smith
stevensmithvo@gmail.com
www.classicbooksexplained.com

WHY DO STUDENTS STUDY SHAKESPEARE'S HAMLET

Shakespeare's "Hamlet" is studied by students for a number of reasons, many of which revolve around its cultural significance, deep exploration of human nature, masterful use of language, and complexity of themes. Here are some reasons in greater detail:

1. **Cultural Significance**: As one of William Shakespeare's most renowned tragedies, "Hamlet" holds a significant place in Western literature and global culture. Many phrases from the play have entered common usage, such as "to be or not to be," "there's something rotten in the state of Denmark," and "frailty, thy name is woman." Understanding these references requires knowledge of the play, and studying "Hamlet" allows students to gain a deeper understanding of their cultural heritage.

2. **Language and Literary Techniques**: Shakespeare's use of language in "Hamlet" is considered some of his finest work. The play provides numerous examples of various literary devices, including metaphor, simile, personification, irony, and dramatic monologue. Studying "Hamlet" helps students develop a greater appreciation for these techniques and enhance their understanding of English literature.

1. **Exploration of Human Nature**: "Hamlet" delves deeply into various aspects of human nature, including the conflict between reason and emotion, the nature of madness, and the effects of guilt and revenge. Studying these themes can help students develop their understanding of psychology and philosophy, and apply these concepts to their own lives.

2. **Character Development and Analysis**: The characters in "Hamlet" are complex, multifaceted, and undergo significant development throughout the play. Studying these characters helps students learn how to analyze and understand character development, motivation, and interactions.

3. **Plot Structure and Dramatic Elements**: "Hamlet" is a masterclass in dramatic structure, with its engaging plot, dramatic irony, and suspense. Students studying the play can gain insights into how stories are crafted and what makes a narrative engaging and meaningful.

4. **Examination of Societal Issues**: "Hamlet" raises many questions about society and morality, including issues related to power, corruption, morality, and gender roles. These themes are as relevant today as they were in Shakespeare's time, and studying them can help students develop a broader perspective on society.

5. **Critical Thinking and Interpretation Skills**: The complexity of "Hamlet" necessitates careful reading and interpretation. Studying the play encourages students to think critically and analyze the text from various perspectives. This can aid in the development of their reasoning and argumentation skills.

1. **Historical Context**: "Hamlet" also offers insight into the historical period in which it was written, the late Elizabethan era. Studying the play can help students understand the social, political, and cultural dynamics of the time, providing a real-world context to historical study.

In summary, studying "Hamlet" provides students with a rich and multifaceted learning experience, stretching their analytical skills, expanding their cultural and historical knowledge, and offering profound insights into the human condition.

Cultural Significance of Hamlet

"Hamlet" is arguably one of the most influential works of literature in Western culture, and it has a wide-reaching cultural significance. Here is an in-depth examination:

1. **Iconic Phrases**: Several phrases and expressions coined in "Hamlet" have entered the English language and are still in widespread use today. Expressions such as "To be or not to be," "the slings and arrows of outrageous fortune," "to thine own self be true," and "there's something rotten in the state of Denmark" have become a part of the cultural lexicon, frequently referenced in literature, films, speeches, and everyday conversation. Even those who have never read or seen the play are likely to recognize these phrases.

2. **Global Reach**: "Hamlet" has been translated into almost every language and performed more often than any other play around the world. It's not just the English-speaking world that has been influenced by "Hamlet"; the play has been adapted in numerous cultures, taking on different interpretations and significances. For example, it has been reimagined in Japan in the form of Noh theater (Yukio Ninagawa's "Noh Hamlet"), and its themes of political corruption and personal revenge have found resonance in many societies.

1. **Literary Influence**: "Hamlet" has influenced countless writers since its first performance. Its themes, characters, and plot have been echoed in novels, plays, and poems over centuries. Writers from Goethe to James Joyce have referenced or responded to "Hamlet" in their works. T.S. Eliot's "The Love Song of J. Alfred Prufrock" includes a reference to Prince Hamlet, and in his essay "Hamlet and His Problems", Eliot notably describes the play as a failure—a controversial stance that nevertheless testifies to Hamlet's central position in literary discourse.

2. **Influence on Cinema and Popular Culture**: "Hamlet" has been adapted numerous times for cinema and television, influencing the way stories are told in these media. The play has been interpreted by renowned directors like Laurence Olivier, Kenneth Branagh, and Franco Zeffirelli, and reimagined in movies like "The Lion King" and "Rosencrantz & Guildenstern Are Dead". The play's iconic soliloquies and dramatic scenes have informed cinematic storytelling techniques.

3. **Existentialism and Philosophy**: "Hamlet" is often interpreted as a deeply philosophical play, posing profound questions about existence, morality, and the nature of the self. Prince Hamlet's famous soliloquy, "To be or not to be", has become a symbol of existential questioning. The play's exploration of these themes has made it a touchstone in philosophical discourse and has shaped Western philosophical thought, especially existentialism. Its influence is visible in the works of philosophers like Kierkegaard, Nietzsche, and Heidegger.

4. **Education**: "Hamlet" holds a significant place in educational curricula around the world. It's often students' first introduction to Shakespeare's tragedies, offering a deep exploration of com-

plex themes like mortality, revenge, and madness. By studying "Hamlet", students are introduced to the richness of Shakespeare's language, the depth of his characterizations, and the complexity of his themes.

5. **Reflection of Societal Issues**: The play's themes, such as political intrigue, moral corruption, revenge, madness, and death, reflect concerns that are timeless and universal. "Hamlet" continues to be relevant because it deals with fundamental human experiences, and it serves as a mirror to the society we live in.

Language and Literary Techniques

Shakespeare's "Hamlet" is a treasure trove of language and literary techniques, showcasing the Bard's virtuosity in crafting engaging and poignant dialogue. Below, some of the key techniques are detailed with reference to specific instances in the play:

1. **Iambic Pentameter**: Like much of Shakespeare's work, "Hamlet" is written largely in iambic pentameter—a line of verse with five pairs of stressed and unstressed syllables. This gives the language a rhythm and musicality, and can also be used to reveal character. Hamlet's famous "To be or not to be" soliloquy (Act 3, Scene 1) is a prominent example of iambic pentameter.

2. **Soliloquies**: "Hamlet" contains some of the most famous soliloquies in the English language. These speeches, delivered by a character when they're alone on stage, give audiences insight into the character's inner thoughts and feelings. Hamlet's soliloquies (like "O, what a rogue and peasant slave am I" in Act 2, Scene 2 and "To be or not to be" in Act 3, Scene 1) are particularly notable for their depth and complexity.

3. **Word Play and Puns**: Shakespeare frequently employs word play and puns to add humor, develop character, and hint at underlying meanings. An example of this can be found in Hamlet's conversation with Polonius (Act 3, Scene 2), where he mockingly calls him a "fishmonger" – a term which was used as slang for a pimp,

thereby hinting at Polonius's manipulative use of his daughter
Ophelia.

4. **Metaphor and Simile**: These figures of speech allow Shakespeare
   to make comparisons that add depth and richness to his language.
   For instance, in Act 3, Scene 1, during the "To be or not to be"
   soliloquy, Hamlet uses a metaphor to describe death as the "undis-
   covered country" from whose "bourne no traveller returns".

5. **Irony**: Shakespeare uses dramatic, situational, and verbal irony
   throughout "Hamlet". One of the most notable uses of dramatic
   irony is the audience's knowledge of Hamlet's feigned madness,
   while other characters remain oblivious (most of the play). Situational irony can be seen when Hamlet kills Polonius (Act 3, Scene
   4) thinking he is Claudius.

6. **Foreshadowing**: Shakespeare uses foreshadowing to hint at fu-
   ture events. An early example is the appearance of the ghost (Act
   1, Scene 1), foreshadowing the tragic events that are to come.

7. **Imagery**: Imagery is used to create vivid mental pictures and
   appeal to the senses of the audience. For example, in Act 1, Scene
   2, Hamlet describes the world as an "unweeded garden" full of
   "things rank and gross in nature", which paints a picture of his
   despair and disgust.

8. **Symbolism**: Shakespeare uses symbols to convey deeper meanings. The ghost, for example, symbolizes the unresolved issues of
   the kingdom and Hamlet's psychological torment.

9. **Double Entendre**: Shakespeare often uses words or phrases that
   have more than one meaning to add complexity to his dialogue.
   Hamlet's exchange with Ophelia in the "Get thee to a nunnery"

scene (Act 3, Scene 1) is filled with sexual double entendre.

Exploration of Human Nature

"Hamlet" is often hailed as Shakespeare's deepest probe into the human psyche, where the exploration of human nature is a significant aspect of the play. It touches upon key facets such as identity, morality, madness, mortality, and existentialism. Here are the in-depth details:

1. **Identity and Selfhood**: The theme of identity is a core aspect of "Hamlet". Shakespeare explores the way in which people perceive themselves and how they portray themselves to others. Hamlet struggles with his identity throughout the play, seen notably in his soliloquy "To be, or not to be" (Act 3, Scene 1), where he contemplates life, death, and the authenticity of his own existence.

2. **Madness**: The theme of madness is a pivotal element in the play. Hamlet's "antic disposition" (Act 1, Scene 5) raises the question of his sanity. This feigned madness becomes a tool for Hamlet to safely express his disgust for his mother's hasty marriage and his contempt for Claudius. Ophelia's descent into actual madness, culminating in her suicide, stands in contrast to Hamlet's feigned insanity, revealing Shakespeare's exploration of mental illness and the effects of grief and despair.

3. **Morality and Ethics**: Hamlet's contemplation of revenge and murder puts moral questions at the forefront. He struggles with the moral legitimacy of avenging his father's murder by killing Claudius, wrestling with questions of right and wrong, justice and

revenge. This internal moral conflict is evident in his soliloquies, notably in Act 3, Scene 3, where he has the chance to kill Claudius but refrains because Claudius is in prayer.

4. **Mortality and the Fear of Death**: Death and the fear of the unknown are central to the play. The death of King Hamlet sets the events of the play in motion, and Hamlet's contemplation of his own death ("To be, or not to be" soliloquy, Act 3, Scene 1) reflects a profound existential anxiety. The theme of mortality is further explored through the graveyard scene (Act 5, Scene 1), where Hamlet holds the skull of Yorick, contemplating the inevitability of death.

5. **Existentialism**: "Hamlet" grapples with existential issues about the meaning of life and the individual's place in the universe. Hamlet's internal conflict and contemplation of suicide reveal an individual in crisis, grappling with the apparent futility and absurdity of existence.

These aspects of human nature explored in "Hamlet" have been extensively analyzed and referenced in various works of literary criticism and psychoanalytic studies, including:

- Alexander, P. (Ed.). (1951). "Hamlet, Prince of Denmark". The Complete Works of Shakespeare. London: Collins.

- Bloom, H. (2003). "Hamlet: Poem Unlimited". Riverhead Books.

- Freud, S. (1953). "The Interpretation of Dreams". In J. Strachey (Ed. and Trans.), The Standard Edition of the Complete Psychological Works of Sigmund Freud (Vol. 4). Hogarth Press. (Original work published 1899).

- Greenblatt, S. (2004). "Hamlet in Purgatory". Princeton University Press.

- Jones, E. (1976). "Hamlet and Oedipus". Norton. (Original work published 1949).

CHARACTER DEVELOPMENT AND ANALYSIS

"Hamlet" boasts an array of complex characters who undergo significant development throughout the play. Here's a look at some of the main characters:

1. **Hamlet**: The Prince of Denmark, Hamlet is a complex character who undergoes significant development. His journey begins with grief over his father's death and anger at his mother's quick remarriage. He then feigns madness to investigate his father's murder. Hamlet's philosophical reflections, such as the famous "To be or not to be" soliloquy (Act 3, Scene 1), reflect his deep existential anxiety and contemplation of death. By the end of the play, Hamlet seems to have come to terms with his fate, accepting his impending death with a newfound stoicism (Act 5, Scene 2).

2. **Claudius**: Claudius starts as a confident, manipulative king who has usurped his brother's throne and married his widow. However, as the play progresses and Hamlet's feigned madness and Claudius's guilt over his fratricide intensify, Claudius becomes increasingly paranoid and fearful, resorting to more desperate measures to protect his power, including attempts to murder Hamlet (Act 4, Scene 3).

3. **Gertrude**: Gertrude's character development is more subtle but still significant. She begins the play seemingly complicit in Claudius's deeds, but as the play progresses, she becomes increas-

ingly conflicted and confused. Her interactions with Hamlet, particularly in the closet scene (Act 3, Scene 4), show her wrestling with her actions and her loyalty to both Claudius and her son.

4. **Ophelia**: Ophelia begins as a dutiful daughter, submissive to the wills of her father and brother. However, following Hamlet's rejection and the death of her father, Ophelia descends into madness. This transformation offers a tragic look at the consequences of the powerlessness and repression Ophelia experiences.

5. **Polonius**: Polonius is initially presented as a somewhat comical character, known for his long-winded speeches and tendency to state the obvious. However, as the play progresses, he is revealed to be politically shrewd and manipulative, using his own daughter to spy on Hamlet (Act 2, Scene 1). His accidental death at the hands of Hamlet (Act 3, Scene 4) triggers a series of tragic events.

These characters and their development are extensively analyzed in numerous literary criticism and academic studies. For further reference, consider these sources:

- Alexander, P. (Ed.). (1951). "Hamlet, Prince of Denmark". The Complete Works of Shakespeare. London: Collins.

- Bloom, H. (2003). "Hamlet: Poem Unlimited". Riverhead Books.

- Showalter, E. (1985). "Representing Ophelia: Women, Madness, and the Responsibilities of Feminist Criticism". In "Shakespeare and the Question of Theory", edited by Patricia Parker and Geoffrey Hartman. New York: Methuen.

- Lacan, J. (2001). "Desire and the Interpretation of Desire in Hamlet". In "Literature and Psychoanalysis", edited by Shoshana Felman. Johns Hopkins University Press.

Plot Structure and Dramatic Elements

"Hamlet" is a tragedy that follows a clear dramatic structure, comprising five acts that include exposition, rising action, climax, falling action, and denouement.

1. **Exposition (Act 1)**: The play opens with the appearance of the ghost of King Hamlet to the sentinels. Prince Hamlet learns from the ghost that his father was murdered by Claudius, Hamlet's uncle. Hamlet swears to avenge his father's death.

2. **Rising Action (Acts 2 and 3)**: Hamlet feigns madness as part of his plan to investigate his father's murder. He rejects Ophelia, causing her distress, and stages a play, "The Mousetrap," to confirm Claudius's guilt. The climax is reached in Act 3, Scene 3 when Hamlet refrains from killing Claudius while he prays.

3. **Climax (Act 3, Scene 4)**: Hamlet confronts his mother, Gertrude, in her closet and kills Polonius, who was hiding behind the arras. The ghost appears again, reminding Hamlet of his quest for revenge and to spare his mother.

4. **Falling Action (Act 4)**: Hamlet is sent to England with Rosencrantz and Guildenstern, who carry a letter from Claudius ordering Hamlet's execution. Hamlet discovers the plot and returns to Denmark, while Rosencrantz and Guildenstern proceed to their deaths. Ophelia, driven mad by Hamlet's rejection and her father's

death, drowns. Laertes, Polonius's son, vows revenge on Hamlet.

5. **Denouement (Act 5)**: In the final act, a duel between Hamlet and Laertes takes place, arranged by Claudius who plans to kill Hamlet. The duel ends in disaster, with Gertrude accidentally drinking poisoned wine intended for Hamlet, and Laertes and Hamlet wounding each other with a poisoned sword. As he dies, Hamlet kills Claudius. Fortinbras of Norway arrives to claim the Danish throne.

This play also employs several dramatic elements:

Foreshadowing: The ghost's revelation of his murder foreshadows Hamlet's quest for revenge.

Dramatic Irony: The audience knows many things that the characters do not. For example, we know of the murder when Claudius and Gertrude do not. We are also aware of Hamlet's feigned madness when other characters are not.

Comic Relief: The gravediggers in Act 5 provide comic relief with their humorous banter, serving to lighten the tragic mood of the play.

Soliloquies: Hamlet's soliloquies give insight into his thoughts and feelings, such as his contemplation of life and death in the "To be, or not to be" soliloquy.

Symbolism: Several objects and actions symbolize broader concepts. The ghost symbolizes unfinished business and revenge, while Yorick's skull symbolizes death and the futility of life.

References for these points can be found in the following works:

- Alexander, P. (Ed.). (1951). "Hamlet, Prince of Denmark". The Complete Works of Shakespeare. London: Collins.

- Bloom, H. (2003). "Hamlet: Poem Unlimited". Riverhead Books.

- Prosser, E. (1967). "Hamlet and Revenge". Stanford University

Press.

- Greenblatt, S. (2004). "Will in the World: How Shakespeare Became Shakespeare". Norton.

Examination of Societal Issues

"Hamlet" is not only a play about individual characters and their personal tragedies but also a critique and exploration of broader societal issues. These include the political intrigue and power struggle, the role and treatment of women, the ethics of revenge and murder, and the effects of corruption. Here are some of these issues in more detail:

1. **Political Intrigue and Power Struggle**: "Hamlet" reveals the dark side of political power. Claudius's fratricide and subsequent usurpation of the throne highlight the lengths individuals will go for power. The political instability of Denmark, represented by Fortinbras's impending invasion, reflects how power struggles and political corruption can destabilize an entire kingdom.

2. **The Role and Treatment of Women**: The two female characters, Gertrude and Ophelia, provide a lens through which to examine the status and treatment of women. They are largely controlled by the male characters and face tragic ends, suggesting a critique of a patriarchal society that confines and marginalizes women.

3. **Ethics of Revenge and Murder**: Hamlet's dilemma over avenging his father's murder by killing Claudius throws light on the ethical quandaries surrounding revenge and murder. This theme raises questions about the nature of justice and the moral boundaries individuals may cross in the pursuit of it.

4. **Effects of Corruption**: The ghost describes the entire state of Denmark as an "unweeded garden" (Act 1, Scene 2) that has fallen into disarray due to Claudius's immoral actions. This metaphor suggests a critique of the broader societal corruption that can stem from the actions of those in power.

These societal issues and themes have been the subject of numerous critical analyses and scholarly studies, including:

- Adelman, J. (1992). "Suffocating Mothers: Fantasies of Maternal Origin in Shakespeare's Plays". Routledge.

- Greenblatt, S. (2001). "Hamlet in Purgatory". Princeton University Press.

- Newell, A. (2015). "Passions in Hamlet". Cambridge University Press.

- Smith, R. (2004). "A Heart Cleft in Twain: The Dilemma of Shakespeare's Gertrude". In "The Woman's Part: Feminist Criticism of Shakespeare", edited by Carolyn Ruth Swift Lenz, Gayle Greene, and Carol Thomas Neely. University of Illinois Press.

CRITICAL THINKING AND INTERPRETATION SKILLS

"Hamlet" provides a rich text for honing critical thinking and interpretation skills. The complex plot, rich language, and multi-faceted characters offer abundant opportunities for analysis and interpretation. Here are some ways studying "Hamlet" can help develop these skills:

1. **Critical Reading**: The play demands a high level of attention to details, including Shakespeare's use of language, literary techniques, and allusions. Readers must discern the literal and figurative meanings of complex dialogue and soliloquies.

2. **Interpretation**: There's a range of interpretations possible for almost every aspect of "Hamlet". Is Hamlet truly mad, or is it entirely an act? Is the ghost a reliable source of information? How should we understand Hamlet's inaction? Every reader might form their unique interpretation of these questions, fostering their ability to think independently and draw personal conclusions from the text.

3. **Evaluation of Sources and Evidence**: Hamlet is a character surrounded by uncertainty. This demands readers to question the reliability of characters and their statements, similar to evaluating sources and evidence in a critical thinking context.

4. **Understanding Context**: The ability to think critically about

the historical, social, and cultural contexts of "Hamlet" provides valuable insight into the play's themes and messages. For instance, understanding the Elizabethan beliefs about ghosts, death, and the afterlife can shed light on Hamlet's reactions and the play's overarching themes.

5. **Synthesis**: The play asks readers to synthesize information from various sources, including the text itself, historical context, and other scholarly interpretations. This synthesis is crucial to forming a well-rounded understanding of the play.

6. **Argumentation**: "Hamlet" is the subject of numerous debates in literary scholarship. Engaging with these debates—whether about Hamlet's character, the play's themes, or its cultural impact—encourages the development of argumentation skills, including the ability to support interpretations with evidence from the text.

For a deeper understanding of these concepts, you may refer to:

- Bloom, H. (2003). "Hamlet: Poem Unlimited". Riverhead Books. This offers various interpretations of the play's elements.

- Eagleton, T. (1986). "William Shakespeare". In "The Eagleton Reader", edited by Stephen Regan. Blackwell. This work can help understand the political and social context of Shakespeare's works.

- Greenblatt, S. (2004). "Will in the World: How Shakespeare Became Shakespeare". Norton. This can provide context on Shakespeare's life and times.

- Foster, T. (2003). "How to Read Literature Like a Professor: A Lively and Entertaining Guide to Reading Between the Lines". HarperCollins. This can help develop literary interpretation skills.

HISTORICAL CONTEXT

"Hamlet," written between 1599 and 1601, is a product of the Elizabethan era in England, a time when Queen Elizabeth I ruled (1558–1603). Understanding the historical context of this period is crucial to appreciating and interpreting the play.

Politics and Power: The Elizabethan era was a time of political intrigue, with power struggles both within England and with other nations. Shakespeare reflects this in the fraught political atmosphere of "Hamlet", where the throne is won through deceit and murder, and the state of Denmark is threatened by external invasion.

Religion: The Elizabethan era was marked by religious tensions. England had recently broken with the Catholic Church under Henry VIII and established the Protestant Church of England under Elizabeth I. This period saw ongoing conflicts between Catholics and Protestants. In "Hamlet", the ghost's existence in a purgatory-like state reflects a Catholic concept, while the players' performance in the court and Claudius's private prayer are more aligned with Protestant practices. These religious elements reflect the uncertainty and religious hybridity of Shakespeare's time.

Philosophy and the Human Condition: The Renaissance, which overlapped the Elizabethan era, was a time of great change and new thinking in areas of science, philosophy, and human understanding. In "Hamlet", we see the influence of Renaissance humanism in Hamlet's introspective exploration of mortality, existence, and the human condition. His soliloquy "To be, or not to be" can be seen as a reflection of the philosophical enquiries that typified the Renaissance.

Theatre: The Elizabethan era was a golden age for English theatre. Shakespeare's plays, including "Hamlet", were written for a broad audience, ranging from commoners to nobles. The existence of a play within the play ("The Mousetrap") may also reflect contemporary theatrical practices and its role in society.

For further reading on the historical context of "Hamlet", these sources provide comprehensive information:

- Greenblatt, S. (2004). "Will in the World: How Shakespeare Became Shakespeare". Norton.

- Palfrey, B., and Archer, J. (2015). "Shakespeare in Context". Cambridge University Press.

- Wilson, R. (2004). "Secrets of the Elizabethan Court". In "Shakespeare: The Evidence: Unlocking the Mysteries of the Man and His Work". St. Martin's Press.

- Yates, F. (2015). "The Occult Philosophy in the Elizabethan Age". Routledge.

HAMLET SUMMARY

"Hamlet" is a complex and multi-layered tragedy by William Shakespeare. Here is a detailed summary of each act:

Act 1:

The play begins on the ramparts of Elsinore Castle in Denmark with guards who have seen a ghost resembling the late King Hamlet. When Prince Hamlet visits the ramparts, the ghost appears and reveals that he was murdered by his brother, Claudius, who has now taken the throne and married Hamlet's mother, Gertrude. The ghost commands Hamlet to seek revenge. Disturbed by this revelation, Hamlet swears to avenge his father's death.

Act 2:

As part of his plan, Hamlet feigns madness to throw off suspicion. Concerned about Hamlet's erratic behavior, Claudius and Gertrude enlist Hamlet's friends, Rosencrantz and Guildenstern, to spy on him. Meanwhile, Polonius, the king's advisor, believes that Hamlet's madness is due to unrequited love for his daughter, Ophelia. Hamlet, in his "mad" state, criticizes Polonius and rejects Ophelia. A troupe of actors arrives at the castle, and Hamlet requests them to perform a specific play, "The Murder of Gonzago," with added lines that closely mirror the murder of his father.

Act 3:

The play-within-a-play takes place, and as Hamlet hoped, it provokes a guilty reaction from Claudius. Confirming Claudius's guilt, Hamlet resolves to kill him but finds Claudius in prayer and decides not to, believing that killing him while he prays would send his soul to heaven. Hamlet confronts his mother about her hasty marriage to Claudius and accidentally kills Polonius, who was hiding behind a tapestry. The ghost reappears, reminding Hamlet to focus on revenge and to leave his mother's fate to heaven.

Act 4:

Hamlet's actions lead Claudius to send him to England with secret orders for his execution. However, Hamlet discovers the plot and escapes, arranging for the execution of Rosencrantz and Guildenstern instead. In Elsinore, Ophelia, driven mad by Hamlet's rejection and her father's death, drowns. Laertes, Polonius's son, returns from France, determined to avenge his father's and sister's deaths.

Act 5:

Back in Denmark, Hamlet encounters a gravedigger and contemplates death. He comes across a funeral procession and realizes it is for Ophelia. Grief-stricken and enraged, he confronts Laertes. Claudius, seizing the opportunity, arranges a fencing match between Hamlet and Laertes, planning to poison Hamlet during the match. The plan goes awry; Gertrude accidentally drinks the poisoned wine intended for Hamlet, and both Laertes and Hamlet are wounded with the poisoned sword. As he dies, Laertes reconciles with Hamlet and reveals Claudius's plot. Hamlet then stabs Claudius and forces him to drink the remaining poisoned wine, finally fulfilling his revenge. As Hamlet dies, he names Prince Fortinbras of Norway as his chosen successor. Fortinbras arrives, orders a military funeral for Hamlet, and claims the Danish throne.

Themes of the play

"Hamlet" explores several major themes, which have been subjects of extensive scholarly interpretation. Here are some key themes:

1. **Revenge and Justice**: The central theme of "Hamlet" is the moral legitimacy and consequences of revenge. Hamlet's pursuit of revenge against Claudius is the driving force of the play. Yet, this desire for revenge creates a moral ambiguity, as it pushes Hamlet towards actions that could be perceived as unjust or immoral.

Reference: Kerrigan, W. (1996). "Revenge Tragedy: Aeschylus to Armageddon". Oxford University Press.

2. **Mortality and the Meaning of Life**: Hamlet's soliloquy in Act 3, Scene 1 is a profound meditation on life, death, and what lies beyond: "To be, or not to be: that is the question: Whether 'tis nobler in the mind to suffer The slings and arrows of outrageous fortune, Or to take arms against a sea of troubles, And by opposing end them?" These lines embody his contemplation of mortality and the meaning of life. Hamlet's existential questions reflect the human struggle with mortality and the search for life's purpose.

Reference: Greenblatt, S. (2004). "Hamlet in Purgatory". Princeton University Press.

3. **Madness and Sanity**: Hamlet's feigned madness is a major theme. In Act 2, Scene 2, he declares, "I am but mad

north-north-west: when the wind is southerly, I know a hawk from a handsaw." Hamlet's feigned madness—and possibly actual descent into madness—coupled with Ophelia's breakdown, forms a recurrent theme in the play. The play constantly questions the line between sanity and insanity.

Reference: Neely, C.T. (1980). "Documents in Madness: Reading Madness and Gender in Shakespeare's Tragedies and Early Modern Culture". Shakespeare Quarterly, 42(3), 291-314.

4. **Deception and Appearance vs. Reality**: Deception is a recurring theme in "Hamlet". This theme is apparent throughout, highlighted in Act 1, Scene 2, when Hamlet says, "Seems, madam! Nay, it is; I know not 'seems'." Characters often hide their true intentions or feelings, creating a disparity between appearance and reality. The concept of "seeming" versus "being" is continually explored. Reference: Bloom, H. (2003). "Hamlet: Poem Unlimited". Riverhead Books.

5. **Corruption and Disease**: This theme is symbolically represented throughout the play. In Act 1, Scene 2, Hamlet declares: "Things rank and gross in nature Possess it merely. That it should come to this!" The murder of King Hamlet and Claudius's usurpation of the throne serve as symbols of moral and political corruption infecting Denmark, often metaphorically referred to as disease or poison.

Reference: Bowers, F. (1964). "Hamlet as Minister and Scourge". PMLA, 79(4), 448-459.

6. **Inaction and Delay**: Hamlet's delay or procrastination in avenging his father's death forms a significant theme of the play, best exemplified in his soliloquy in Act 3, Scene 1: "Thus conscience does make cowards of us all; And thus the native hue of resolution

Is sicklied o'er with the pale cast of thought...". This inaction raises questions about Hamlet's character, will, and the human condition.

Reference: Shapiro, J. (2010). "A Year in the Life of William Shakespeare: 1599". Harper Perennial.

7. **The Nature of Ghosts and the Supernatural:** The ghost of Hamlet's father plays a significant role in the play, introducing the theme of the supernatural. This is evident from Act 1, Scene 5: "I am thy father's spirit, Doomed for a certain term to walk the night..."

Each of these themes contributes to the play's enduring relevance and the rich diversity of interpretations it has inspired over centuries.

What are the symbolisms in Hamlet

"Hamlet" by William Shakespeare contains a wealth of symbolism that deepens the play's themes and characterizations. Here are some prominent symbols in the play with references:

1. **The Ghost**: The ghost of King Hamlet symbolizes the unsettled matters of the kingdom and the corruption that Claudius has brought upon Denmark. It's a reminder of the unavenged murder that has disrupted the natural order.

2. **Yorick's Skull**: The skull of Yorick, the court jester from Hamlet's childhood, represents mortality and the inevitable fate of all humans. When Hamlet holds the skull in the graveyard scene, he reflects on the vanity of life: "Alas, poor Yorick! I knew him, Horatio: a fellow / of infinite jest, of most excellent fancy" (Act 5, Scene 1).

3. **The Poisoned Sword and Wine**: The poisoned sword and wine in the final scene symbolize deceit and treachery. Claudius uses both to try to kill Hamlet, but ironically, these instruments lead to his own death as well as the deaths of Gertrude, Laertes, and Hamlet.

4. **The Mousetrap Play**: The play within a play that Hamlet arranges symbolizes the hidden truths beneath surface appearances. By reenacting King Hamlet's murder, it reveals Claudius's

guilt: "The play's the thing / Wherein I'll catch the conscience of the king" (Act 2, Scene 2).

5. **Ophelia's Flowers**: The flowers Ophelia distributes during her madness each symbolize the various characters and their actions. For instance, fennel and columbines, which she gives to Claudius, are often interpreted as symbols of flattery and unfaithfulness, respectively (Act 4, Scene 5).

6. **Fortinbras and Norway**: The character of Fortinbras and the country of Norway function symbolically as contrasts to Hamlet and Denmark. Where Hamlet hesitates, Fortinbras takes action, and where Denmark is in a state of moral decay, Norway appears more stable and ordered.

7. **Hamlet's "antic disposition"**: Hamlet's feigned madness serves as a symbol of the chaotic state of Denmark and the madness that is, in a sense, catching—first affecting Hamlet, then Ophelia, and then the state as a whole.

These symbols in "Hamlet" serve to illuminate the deeper psychological states of characters, intensify thematic concerns, and enrich the overall reading and interpretative experience of the play.

References are from the text of "Hamlet" by William Shakespeare. For further analysis of the symbolism in "Hamlet", refer to critical works such as "Hamlet's Mill: An Essay Investigating the Origins of Human Knowledge and Its Transmission Through Myth" by Giorgio de Santillana and Hertha von Dechend.

WHO ARE THE IMPORTANT CHARACTERS

"Hamlet" is full of significant characters, each contributing to the play's intricate plot. Here are some of the most important:

1. **Hamlet**: The Prince of Denmark, and the play's protagonist. He is called upon by his father's ghost to avenge his murder, setting the stage for the tragedy to unfold. Hamlet is a complex character, introspective and philosophical, and his contemplation of life, death, and revenge constitute much of the play's substance.

2. **Claudius**: Hamlet's uncle, who becomes King of Denmark after murdering his brother, King Hamlet, and marrying his brother's widow, Queen Gertrude. Claudius is the primary antagonist in the play.

3. **Gertrude**: Hamlet's mother and the Queen of Denmark. Her hasty marriage to Claudius, soon after King Hamlet's death, distresses her son. She is caught in the middle of the conflict between Hamlet and Claudius.

4. **Polonius**: The Lord Chamberlain of Claudius's court, a pompous and verbose man. He is the father of Ophelia and Laertes.

5. **Ophelia**: Polonius's daughter, who has a romantic relationship with Hamlet. As the plot unfolds, Ophelia's relationship with Hamlet deteriorates, contributing to her eventual madness and

tragic death.

6. **Laertes**: Polonius's son and Ophelia's brother. He spends much of the play in France but returns to Denmark upon hearing of his father's death. He is a parallel to Hamlet in many ways and ultimately becomes an instrument of Claudius's plot against Hamlet.

7. **Horatio**: Hamlet's loyal friend from university, who remains true to Hamlet throughout the play. He is the only main character to survive, and Hamlet entrusts him with the task of telling the tragic tale to the world.

8. **Ghost**: The spirit of Hamlet's deceased father, the former King of Denmark. The Ghost reveals to Hamlet that he was murdered by Claudius, sparking the quest for revenge that drives the play.

9. **Rosencrantz and Guildenstern**: Hamlet's former schoolmates who are commissioned by Claudius to spy on Hamlet. Their betrayal reflects the theme of deceit and mistrust that permeates the play.

Each of these characters plays a crucial role in the unfolding of the play's tragic narrative, and each is a testament to Shakespeare's skill in creating multi-faceted, complex characters.

Describe and analyse Hamlet

Hamlet is one of the most complex and widely studied characters in English literature, a prince caught in a web of familial and political intrigue and faced with profound moral and existential dilemmas. Here is a description and analysis of his character with references to the play:

1. **Hamlet as a Philosopher**: Hamlet is noted for his introspective and philosophical nature. He often poses deep existential questions, most famously in his "To be, or not to be" soliloquy (Act 3, Scene 1), where he meditates on the nature of life, death, and the afterlife. This reflects his deep introspection and his struggle with the moral implications of his revenge mission.

2. **Hamlet and Madness**: Hamlet's sanity is a central concern in the play. After his encounter with the ghost of his father, he adopts a guise of madness ("I perchance hereafter shall think meet / To put an antic disposition on." Act 1, Scene 5), as part of his plan to avenge his father's murder. However, as the play progresses, it becomes increasingly difficult to distinguish between his feigned madness and possible genuine mental distress.

3. **Hamlet and Revenge**: Hamlet is essentially a revenge-tragedy protagonist, tasked by his father's ghost to avenge his murder. However, unlike typical revenge heroes, Hamlet is characterised by his indecisiveness and delay. He hesitates to kill Claudius, grappling with moral, ethical, and psychological dilemmas. This is

evident when he spares Claudius while he is praying, fearing that killing him in that state might send him to heaven (Act 3, Scene 3).

4. **Hamlet and his Relationships**: Hamlet's relationships with other characters are complex and layered. His relationship with his mother, Gertrude, is tainted by disgust and disappointment due to her hasty remarriage ("Frailty, thy name is woman!" Act 1, Scene 2). His interactions with Ophelia range from declarations of love to cruel rejections, which play a part in her subsequent madness. His friendship with Horatio is one of the few honest and loyal relationships he has, serving as a stark contrast to the treachery and deceit he experiences from others.

5. **Hamlet as a Tragic Hero**: Hamlet embodies many qualities of a tragic hero: he is a noble character with a tragic flaw (his indecisiveness) that leads to his downfall. Despite his tragic end, Hamlet does fulfill his purpose—avenging his father's murder ("Here, thou incestuous, murderous, damned Dane, / Drink off this potion." Act 5, Scene 2)—though at the cost of nearly every major character's life.

References are from the text of "Hamlet" by William Shakespeare. In-depth analysis of Hamlet's character can also be found in critical works such as "Hamlet and His Problems" by T.S. Eliot and "The Tragic Hero and his Shadow" by Murray Krieger.

DESCRIBE AND ANALYSE CLAUDIUS

Claudius, the antagonist of "Hamlet", is a complex character who uses his political shrewdness and manipulative tactics to maintain his position as the King of Denmark. Here's a detailed analysis of his character with references to the play:

1. **Claudius as a Usurper**: Claudius is the younger brother of King Hamlet, whom he murders to usurp the throne. He solidifies his claim to the throne by hastily marrying Gertrude, the Queen, a move that earns him Hamlet's scorn. His fratricide is revealed when he reacts to the play within the play, thereby confirming the Ghost's story: "Give me some light. Away!" (Act 3, Scene 2).

2. **Claudius as a Manipulator**: Claudius exhibits a highly manipulative nature. He effectively uses courtiers Rosencrantz and Guildenstern to spy on Hamlet (Act 2, Scene 2), and manipulates Laertes into challenging Hamlet to a duel to avenge his father's death (Act 4, Scene 7). These actions reveal his cunning nature and his resolve to maintain power at all costs.

3. **Claudius's Guilt**: Despite his initial ruthless pursuit of power, Claudius shows signs of guilt for his crimes. In a rare moment of introspection, he admits his guilt and attempts to pray for forgiveness: "O, my offence is rank, it smells to heaven; / It hath the primal eldest curse upon't, / A brother's murder." (Act 3, Scene 3). However, he acknowledges that he's unwilling to give up what

he gained from the murder, thus displaying the internal conflict within him.

4. **Claudius as a Politician**: Claudius is a savvy politician, capable of maintaining the support of the court and managing the affairs of the state, as demonstrated by his diplomatic handling of the threat from Fortinbras (Act 1, Scene 2). This political acumen allows him to maintain his hold on the throne, despite the sinister means by which he obtained it.

5. **Claudius's Downfall**: Claudius's downfall is ultimately brought about by his own manipulative schemes when he plans the poisoned duel between Laertes and Hamlet. His machinations backfire, leading to his death and a power vacuum in the state: "Here, thou incestuous, murderous, damned Dane, / Drink off this potion." (Act 5, Scene 2).

Claudius, thus, is not just a one-dimensional villain; he is a deeply flawed character with a balance of traits that make him intriguing and contribute to the overall tragedy of the play.

References are from the text of "Hamlet" by William Shakespeare. In-depth analysis of Claudius's character can be found in critical works like "Shakespeare's Tragic Villains" by William Fitton.

Describe and analyse Gertrude

Gertrude is the Queen of Denmark and mother to Hamlet. Her character is significant in the play, but she is somewhat enigmatic, as Shakespeare offers less insight into her inner thoughts and motivations compared to other main characters. Nevertheless, here is a description and analysis of her character with references to the play:

1. **Gertrude and Her Relationships**: Gertrude's relationships with the two most important men in her life, her husband King Claudius and her son Hamlet, are central to the play. She marries Claudius soon after her first husband's death, a decision that causes tension between her and Hamlet. Hamlet is deeply hurt by what he perceives as her disloyalty, and he confronts her in her closet: "Frailty, thy name is woman!" (Act 1, Scene 2).

2. **Gertrude's Loyalty**: Gertrude is shown to be loyal to Claudius, defending him to Hamlet and doing his bidding throughout the play. However, her motivations for this loyalty are unclear. Some interpretations suggest that she is completely unaware of Claudius's treachery, while others propose that she may know more than she lets on.

3. **Gertrude's Innocence or Guilt**: One of the major ambiguities in "Hamlet" is whether Gertrude shares in Claudius's guilt for the murder of her first husband. The ghost in Hamlet's first encounter makes a suggestive comment: "But virtue, as it never will

be moved, / Though lewdness court it in a shape of heaven, / So lust, though to a radiant angel linked, / Will sate itself in a celestial bed / And prey on garbage" (Act 1, Scene 5), but it stops short of directly accusing her.

4. **Gertrude's Death**: Gertrude's death in the final act is symbolic of the tragic cost of the machinations and deceit that have unfolded. Despite Claudius's warning, she drinks from the poisoned cup intended for Hamlet, showing her loyalty to her son: "I will, my lord; I pray you, pardon me" (Act 5, Scene 2). Her death adds to the dramatic climax of the play and accelerates the tragic end.

5. **Gertrude as a Mother**: Despite the tension, Gertrude consistently shows concern for Hamlet's well-being, suggesting a deep maternal affection. She reports to Claudius on Hamlet's madness with genuine worry: "Mad as the sea and wind, when both contend / Which is the mightier." (Act 4, Scene 1).

Gertrude is a more passive character compared to others in the play. Yet, her role is vital, as it adds complexity to the interpersonal dynamics and contributes significantly to the tragic outcome.

References are from the text of "Hamlet" by William Shakespeare. Further exploration of Gertrude's character can be found in critical works like "Interpreting Gertrude" by Elaine Showalter.

DESCRIBE AND ANALYSE POLONIUS

Polonius, the Lord Chamberlain of Claudius's court, is a significant character in "Hamlet". He's often seen as a comic figure because of his long-winded and convoluted speeches, but his actions have a significant impact on the play's plot and its tragic outcome. Here's a detailed analysis of his character with references to the play:

1. **Polonius as a Manipulator**: Similar to Claudius, Polonius is a manipulative character. He has a strong desire for control and often spies on others, including his own children. He sends Reynaldo to spy on his son Laertes in France (Act 2, Scene 1), and he eavesdrops on Hamlet's conversation with his daughter Ophelia (Act 3, Scene 1).

2. **Polonius's Relationship with His Children**: Polonius is the father of Ophelia and Laertes, and his relationships with them are characterized by control and advice, often unsolicited. His famous speech to Laertes, which includes the advice, "Give thy thoughts no tongue, / Nor any unproportioned thought his act" and "to thine own self be true" (Act 1, Scene 3), while seemingly wise, is delivered in a preachy, overbearing manner.

3. **Polonius and Court Intrigue**: Polonius is deeply involved in court politics. He is a loyal counselor to Claudius, always ready to carry out the king's wishes. His overzealous involvement in court intrigues, however, leads to his tragic death when he hides behind

the arras in Gertrude's room to spy on Hamlet and Gertrude's conversation (Act 3, Scene 4).

4. **Polonius as a Comic Relief**: Polonius provides comic relief with his verbose and often nonsensical speeches. This is evident when he rambles about the cause of Hamlet's madness, saying, "Your noble son is mad. / Mad call I it, for, to define true madness, / What is't but to be nothing else but mad?" (Act 2, Scene 2).

5. **Polonius's Impact on the Plot**: Despite being a seemingly secondary character, Polonius's actions, particularly his decision to use Ophelia to find out more about Hamlet's condition, significantly contribute to the tragedy. His death is the turning point of the play that escalates the conflict between Hamlet and Claudius.

Polonius, therefore, while often perceived as a buffoon due to his talkative nature and penchant for espionage, plays a crucial role in the unfolding tragedy in "Hamlet".

References are from the text of "Hamlet" by William Shakespeare. For further analysis of Polonius's character, you can refer to critical studies such as "Hamlet and the Acting of Revenge" by Peter Mercer.

DESCRIBE AND ANALYSE OPHELIA

Ophelia is one of the main female characters in "Hamlet," who is often viewed as tragic and pitiable. She is the daughter of Polonius and sister of Laertes, and she has a romantic relationship with Prince Hamlet. Here's a detailed analysis of her character:

1. **Ophelia's Submission**: Ophelia is frequently guided, if not manipulated, by the men in her life, including her father, Polonius, and brother, Laertes. They both instruct her to stay away from Hamlet due to his apparent unstable condition. "I shall obey, my lord," she says to her father (Act 1, Scene 3). This obedience underscores her lack of agency and reflects the gender dynamics of her time.

2. **Ophelia and Hamlet**: Ophelia's relationship with Hamlet is complicated and tragic. Despite her genuine affection for Hamlet, she becomes an innocent pawn in the hands of her father and Claudius, used to determine the cause of Hamlet's madness. This ultimately leads to her breakdown when Hamlet cruelly rejects her, saying, "Get thee to a nunnery" (Act 3, Scene 1).

3. **Ophelia's Madness**: After the death of her father and Hamlet's rejection, Ophelia descends into madness. This tragic transformation is marked by her singing of seemingly nonsensical songs and distributing flowers, each with symbolic meanings (Act 4, Scene 5). The exact cause of her madness is a topic of debate, but it can

be seen as a result of her multiple traumatic experiences and the oppressive societal forces around her.

4. **Ophelia's Death**: Ophelia's death by drowning, whether accidental or a suicide, marks one of the most poignant moments of the play. Gertrude's description of her death, "Her clothes spread wide, / And, mermaid-like, awhile they bore her up," (Act 4, Scene 7) paints a tragic picture of a young woman destroyed by the world around her.

5. **Ophelia as a Symbol**: Ophelia serves as a symbol of innocence and purity in the play, making her downfall all the more tragic. She also represents the consequences of political and personal machinations on the vulnerable.

Ophelia is a deeply sympathetic character, a tragic figure caught in the machinations of others. Her story adds emotional depth to "Hamlet" and reinforces its themes of madness, deceit, and the tragic consequences of political ambition.

References are from the text of "Hamlet" by William Shakespeare. Further exploration of Ophelia's character can be found in critical works like "Unpicking the Seams: Madness and Gender in Hamlet" by Sarah Hiscock.

Describe and analyse Laertes

Laertes, the son of Polonius and brother to Ophelia, is a secondary character in "Hamlet" but plays a significant role in the play's climax. Here's a detailed analysis of his character with references to the play:

1. **Laertes as a Foil to Hamlet**: Laertes serves as a foil to Hamlet in the play. While both men seek to avenge their fathers' deaths, their approaches are markedly different. Hamlet is philosophical, contemplative, and struggles with inaction, while Laertes is impulsive and quick to action. After learning of his father's death, Laertes immediately returns to Denmark and demands justice, saying, "That drop so low in this regard of honour / To let him feed, without the primy vantage / Revenge should have his teeth in" (Act 4, Scene 7).

2. **Laertes and His Family**: Laertes's relationships with his family members, particularly Ophelia, are characterized by genuine care and concern. He warns Ophelia about Hamlet's romantic advances, advising her to guard her chastity (Act 1, Scene 3). His actions after learning about the deaths of his father and sister further underscore his familial loyalty.

3. **Laertes's Vengeance**: Driven by anger and grief, Laertes becomes a pawn in Claudius's hands and consents to participate in a scheme to kill Hamlet using a poisoned sword (Act 4, Scene 7). This plot ultimately results in his own death as well as that of

Gertrude and Hamlet.

4. **Laertes's Honour**: Even in his pursuit of revenge, Laertes maintains a certain sense of honour. In his dying moments, he reconciles with Hamlet, exchanges forgiveness, and reveals Claudius's treacherous plot: "He is justly served. / It is a poison tempered by himself. / Exchange forgiveness with me, noble Hamlet" (Act 5, Scene 2).

5. **Laertes's Role in the Tragic End**: Through Laertes, Shakespeare explores the destructive cycle of revenge and its consequences. His vengeful actions contribute significantly to the tragic ending of the play.

Laertes, thus, is a complex character whose passion, impulsive actions, and desire for revenge make him a pivotal figure in the progression of the plot in "Hamlet".

References are from the text of "Hamlet" by William Shakespeare. Further analysis of Laertes's character can be found in critical works like "Shakespearean Tragedy" by A.C. Bradley.

DESCRIBE AND ANALYSE HORATIO

Horatio is a significant character in Shakespeare's "Hamlet" serving as Prince Hamlet's closest friend and confidant. He is the one character who remains loyal and truthful to Hamlet throughout the play. Here's a detailed analysis of his character with references to the play:

1. **Horatio as Hamlet's Friend**: From the start, Horatio is presented as a loyal and trustworthy friend to Hamlet. He accompanies the guards in the first act to confirm the appearance of the ghost, which looks like the dead King Hamlet (Act 1, Scene 2). He then honestly reports this encounter to Prince Hamlet. His willingness to face potential danger to serve his friend underlines his loyalty and steadfastness.

2. **Horatio as a Character of Reason**: Horatio is often seen as the voice of reason in the play. He is grounded, sensible, and less driven by emotion compared to other characters. This trait is evident when he advises Hamlet not to follow the ghost, worrying it might lead him to harm: "What if it tempts you toward the flood, my lord, / Or to the dreadful summit of the cliff" (Act 1, Scene 4).

3. **Horatio's Integrity**: Unlike many other characters in the play, Horatio is not involved in any political intrigue and remains a figure of integrity throughout the play. He is neither swayed by the machinations of Claudius nor does he indulge in any dishonesty.

4. **Horatio as the Survivor**: Horatio is one of the few main characters who survives the tragic events of the play. In the final scene, Horatio wishes to die with Hamlet, but Hamlet insists that he live to tell the true story: "Absent thee from felicity awhile, / To tell my story" (Act 5, Scene 2).

5. **Horatio as a Narrative Device**: From a literary perspective, Horatio also serves as a narrative device for Shakespeare, helping to carry the plot forward and provide important information to both Hamlet and the audience. His character also provides a moral lens through which the audience can evaluate other characters' actions.

In "Hamlet", Horatio serves as a stark contrast to the deceit and manipulation prevalent in the Danish court. He embodies loyalty, honesty, and rational thought, thereby anchoring the play amidst its many chaotic and tragic events.

References are from the text of "Hamlet" by William Shakespeare. Further exploration of Horatio's character can be found in critical works like "The Philosophy of Hamlet" by Harold Bloom.

Describe and analyse the Ghost

The Ghost, appearing as the deceased King Hamlet, is a pivotal character in Shakespeare's "Hamlet". Although the ghost has few appearances, its influence on the play's narrative is profound. Here's a detailed analysis of its character with references to the play:

1. **The Ghost as the Catalyst**: The ghost serves as the catalyst for the play's events. In its encounter with Prince Hamlet, it reveals that it was murdered by Claudius and demands Hamlet avenge his death: "If thou didst ever thy dear father love— / Revenge his foul and most unnatural murder" (Act 1, Scene 5). This sets Hamlet on his path of revenge and raises questions about duty, morality, and the afterlife.

2. **The Ghost as a Symbol of Moral Corruption**: The ghost's description of its purgatorial sufferings symbolizes the moral corruption infecting Denmark under Claudius's rule. Its haunting presence underscores the theme of death and decay that permeates the play: "My hour is almost come, / When I to sulphurous and tormenting flames / Must render up myself" (Act 1, Scene 5).

3. **The Ghost's Ambiguity**: Shakespeare introduces an element of ambiguity surrounding the ghost's nature and intentions. Is it a benevolent spirit seeking justice, a malevolent demon trying to manipulate Hamlet, or a hallucination reflecting Hamlet's inner turmoil? This ambiguity contributes to the play's suspense and to

Hamlet's indecision.

4. **The Ghost and Hamlet's Psychological State**: The ghost plays a significant role in exploring Hamlet's psychological state. Its appearances often coincide with Hamlet's extreme emotional states, suggesting a potential link between the apparition and Hamlet's sanity. It's noteworthy that the ghost is also seen by others (Act 1, Scene 1), establishing its objective reality within the play's universe.

5. **The Ghost and Dramatic Irony**: The ghost contributes to the dramatic irony of the play. While the audience and Hamlet are privy to the ghost's claim of Claudius's guilt, other characters remain ignorant, creating tension and suspense throughout the play.

In essence, the ghost in "Hamlet" is more than a supernatural entity. It is a plot device that drives the narrative forward, provides thematic depth, and adds complexity to the play's exploration of issues like revenge, death, and morality.

References are from the text of "Hamlet" by William Shakespeare. For further exploration of the ghost's role, you can refer to critical works such as "Hamlet and the Vision of Darkness" by Rhodri Lewis.

DESCRIBE AND ANALYSE ROSENCRANTZ AND GUILDENSTERN

Rosencrantz and Guildenstern are the least major characters in Shakespeare's "Hamlet", serving as courtiers and childhood friends of Prince Hamlet. They are almost always seen together in the play, and their roles and personalities are largely indistinguishable from each other. Here's a detailed analysis of their characters with references to the play:

1. **Rosencrantz and Guildenstern as Pawns**: Summoned to Elsinore by Claudius and Gertrude, Rosencrantz and Guildenstern are used as pawns to spy on Hamlet and uncover the cause of his apparent madness. They accept this task without much protest: "Both your Majesties / Might, by the sovereign power you have of us, / Put your dread pleasures more into command / Than to entreaty" (Act 2, Scene 2).

2. **Rosencrantz and Guildenstern as Foils to Hamlet**: Their characters serve as a foil to Hamlet, who, despite being caught in similar political machinations, attempts to grapple with the moral implications of his actions. Unlike Hamlet, they do not reflect on their actions' morality, which eventually leads to their tragic end.

3. **Rosencrantz and Guildenstern's Betrayal**: While they are supposedly Hamlet's friends, they willingly participate in Claudius's plans against him. This betrayal further underscores the themes of deceit and dishonesty in the play.

4. **Rosencrantz and Guildenstern's Deaths**: In a twist of fate, they end up being executed in England due to Hamlet's quick thinking and manipulation of the orders originally meant to execute him: "He should the bearers put to sudden death, / Not shriving time allowed" (Act 5, Scene 2). Their deaths represent the dangers and consequences of blind obedience to power.

5. **Rosencrantz and Guildenstern as Comic Relief**: Their interactions with Hamlet and each other often provide comic relief. Their inability to understand Hamlet's philosophical musings and wordplay highlights their lack of intellectual depth compared to Hamlet.

In essence, Rosencrantz and Guildenstern are characters who, despite their minor roles, provide significant insights into the play's exploration of themes such as betrayal, power, manipulation, and the consequences of moral obliviousness.

References are from the text of "Hamlet" by William Shakespeare. For a more in-depth study of these characters, consider Tom Stoppard's "Rosencrantz and Guildenstern Are Dead," a play that explores their characters from a different perspective.

Who are the minor characters

In addition to the main characters, "Hamlet" also includes a number of minor characters who contribute to the overall plot and themes of the play:

1. **Fortinbras**: The young Prince of Norway, whose father was killed by Hamlet's father. He wishes to attack Denmark to avenge his father's honor and reclaim lost lands. He serves as a foil to Hamlet, acting decisively while Hamlet hesitates. He takes the throne of Denmark at the end of the play.

2. **The Gravediggers**: These are two clowns or peasants who dig Ophelia's grave. Their humorous dialogue provides comic relief, but they also explore themes of death and social class.

3. **Osric**: A courtier who delivers the King's fencing challenge to Hamlet, and later serves as the referee for the fencing match between Hamlet and Laertes. His exaggerated courtesy and flamboyant manner serve to satirize courtly behavior.

4. **Marcellus and Bernardo**: The guards who first see the ghost of King Hamlet and inform Horatio about it. Their role primarily serves to introduce the supernatural element in the play.

5. **Voltemand and Cornelius**: Courtiers whom Claudius sends to Norway to persuade the King to prevent Fortinbras from attacking Denmark.

6. **Francisco**: A soldier and guard at Elsinore. He is on duty when the play begins and is relieved by Bernardo.

7. **Reynaldo**: Polonius's servant, who is sent to France to check up on Laertes.

8. **The Players**: A group of actors who perform a play within the play, "The Murder of Gonzago," at Hamlet's request. Their performance serves to reveal Claudius's guilt.

While these characters have smaller roles, they contribute to the depth and richness of the play, further exploring its themes and moving the plot forward.

Detailed references to each conflict

"Hamlet" by William Shakespeare is rich with various forms of conflict—both internal (within a character's mind) and external (between different characters). These conflicts drive the narrative and underscore the drama of the play. Here are the key conflicts in "Hamlet" with references to the play:

1. **Hamlet vs. Claudius**: The primary external conflict in the play is between Hamlet and his uncle (and stepfather), King Claudius. When the ghost of Hamlet's father reveals that Claudius murdered him to usurp the throne, Hamlet becomes consumed with the desire for revenge: "Haste me to know't, that I, with wings as swift / As meditation or the thoughts of love, / May sweep to my revenge" (Act 1, Scene 5).

2. **Hamlet's Internal Conflict**: Hamlet's inner struggle with the morality of revenge, his fear of the unknown (particularly the afterlife), and his anger at his mother for marrying Claudius create intense internal conflict. The most famous manifestation of this is the "To be or not to be" soliloquy where Hamlet contemplates life, death, and the moral implications of suicide (Act 3, Scene 1).

3. **Hamlet vs. Gertrude**: Hamlet has a conflicted relationship with his mother, Gertrude. He feels betrayed by her quick marriage to Claudius after his father's death. In the famous closet scene, he confronts her about her disloyalty to his father, causing a signifi-

cant conflict between them: "O most wicked speed, to post / With such dexterity to incestuous sheets!" (Act 1, Scene 2).

4. **Hamlet vs. Himself (Inaction vs. Action)**: Throughout the play, Hamlet struggles with his propensity for thought and reflection, which often leads to inaction. This internal conflict is reflected in his soliloquy: "Now whether it be / Bestial oblivion, or some craven scruple / Of thinking too precisely on th' event— / A thought which, quartered, hath but one part wisdom / And ever three parts coward" (Act 4, Scene 4).

5. **Hamlet vs. Laertes**: After the deaths of Polonius and Ophelia, Laertes seeks revenge on Hamlet, culminating in a duel that results in both their deaths: "The devil take thy soul!" (Act 5, Scene 2).

6. **Hamlet vs. Rosencrantz and Guildenstern**: Hamlet's former friends, Rosencrantz and Guildenstern, are asked by Claudius to spy on Hamlet, causing a conflict between them: "Were you not sent for? Is it your own inclining? Is it a free visitation?" (Act 2, Scene 2).

Each of these conflicts contributes to the dramatic tension in "Hamlet" and deepens our understanding of the characters, their motivations, and their tragic flaws.

References are from the text of "Hamlet" by William Shakespeare. For a more in-depth exploration of these conflicts, consider reading "The Tragic Vision of Politics: Ethics, Interests and Orders" by Richard Ned Lebow, which touches on the politics and conflicts in Shakespeare's tragedies.

What is the Climax of the Play

The climax of a play is the turning point, the moment of greatest tension or the most critical event in the plot. In "Hamlet" by William Shakespeare, the climax is often identified as the scene in Act 3, Scene 3, when Hamlet has the opportunity to kill Claudius but chooses not to.

In this scene, Hamlet comes across Claudius while he appears to be praying. Hamlet reasons that killing Claudius while he's in prayer would send him to heaven, an undeserved fate for the man who killed his own brother and seized the throne. Hamlet's soliloquy in this scene reads:

"Now might I do it pat, now he is praying;
And now I'll do't. And so he goes to heaven;
And so am I revenged. That would be scann'd:
A villain kills my father; and for that,
I, his sole son, do this same villain send
To heaven." (Act 3, Scene 3)

Hamlet decides to wait for a time when Claudius is engaged in sin so that his soul will be damned, but this moment of hesitation contributes significantly to the tragic unfolding of the events in the play.

While this is a commonly accepted climax, different interpretations may place the climax elsewhere, as the structure of Shakespeare's plays often allows for various moments of heightened tension and drama. Some might argue that the climax is the play-within-the-play in Act 3, Scene 2, when Claudius's guilt is confirmed, or even later in the final act with the tragic duel. This points to the complex structure of "Hamlet" and the multiplicity of interpretations it invites.

Further expanding on the topic of the climax, we can consider these additional points of climax:

The Play-Within-a-Play (Act 3, Scene 2): The staging of "The Mousetrap" represents a significant turning point in the narrative. Hamlet uses the play to "catch the conscience of the king" and confirm his guilt. Claudius's reaction to the play reveals his guilt to Hamlet and the audience, intensifying the conflict between Hamlet and Claudius:

"Give me some light: away!
All: Lights, lights, lights!" (Act 3, Scene 2)

The fact that Claudius cannot bear to watch the play confirms to Hamlet and the audience that Claudius is indeed guilty of murdering King Hamlet.

The Closet Scene (Act 3, Scene 4): The confrontation between Hamlet and Gertrude in Gertrude's private chambers is another crucial moment. Here, Hamlet scolds his mother for her quick marriage to Claudius after King Hamlet's death. The scene escalates when Hamlet accidentally kills Polonius, thinking he is Claudius:

"Thou wretched, rash, intruding fool, farewell!
I took thee for thy better: take thy fortune;
Thou find'st to be too busy is some danger." (Act 3, Scene 4)

This act drastically alters the course of the play. Hamlet's accidental murder of Polonius initiates a series of tragic events, leading to Ophelia's madness and death, Laertes's quest for revenge, and eventually the tragic conclusion in Act 5.

The Final Duel (Act 5, Scene 2): The final duel between Hamlet and Laertes can also be considered a climax due to its high stakes and dramatic tension. It's the moment where all remaining key players die, effectively concluding the narrative:

"I am dead, Horatio. Wretched queen, adieu!
You that look pale and tremble at this chance,
That are but mutes or audience to this act,
Had I but time—as this fell sergeant, Death,
Is strict in his arrest—O, I could tell you—
But let it be." (Act 5, Scene 2)

In each of these moments, the narrative tension reaches a peak, and the course of events is significantly influenced. This multiplicity of climaxes in "Hamlet" is a testament to the richness of Shakespeare's storytelling and the complexity of the play's structure.

WHAT IS THE MORAL OF THE STORY

As with many of Shakespeare's plays, "Hamlet" presents multiple moral lessons rather than one definitive moral. However, here are some significant moral themes that can be gleaned from the play:

1. **The Consequences of Revenge**: One of the key themes of "Hamlet" is the idea that seeking revenge can lead to tragedy. Hamlet's obsession with avenging his father's death drives much of the play's action and ultimately leads to the deaths of many characters, including Hamlet himself. This could suggest a moral lesson about the destructive power of revenge and the danger of letting it consume one's life.

2. **The Danger of Deception**: Deception is another central theme in the play, as nearly every character engages in some form of deceit. This dishonesty breeds mistrust and confusion, leading to tragic misunderstandings and death. The moral here could be a warning about the consequences of dishonesty.

3. **The Complexity of Action and Inaction**: Hamlet's struggle with action and inaction is a critical element of his character and the overall narrative. His inability to act decisively leads to unnecessary death and destruction. Yet, when he does take action, it often results in negative outcomes. This tension suggests a moral about the need for thoughtful, deliberate action rather than impulsive or overly cautious behavior.

4. **The Impermanence of Life**: The recurring contemplation of mortality, especially through Hamlet's soliloquies and the gravedigger scene, communicates a moral lesson about the transient nature of life. Every character, irrespective of their status or deeds, meets the same end: death. This could lead to interpretations about the importance of living a meaningful, ethical life.

5. **Corruption Leads to Downfall**: The moral decay within the state of Denmark, embodied by Claudius's treachery, ultimately leads to its downfall, suggesting a moral lesson about the destructive nature of corruption at both individual and societal levels.

While these morals can be drawn from the play, it's essential to remember that Shakespeare's works are complex and open to multiple interpretations. Different readers may take away different moral lessons based on their reading and interpretation of the text.

WHAT ARE THE FAMOUS QUOTES

"Hamlet" is renowned for its wealth of profound and memorable quotes permeating popular culture and scholarly discourse. Here are some of the most famous quotes from the play, along with references:

1. **"To be, or not to be: that is the question:"** (Act 3, Scene 1)

   - Hamlet's soliloquy contemplating the nature of existence and the appeal of suicide in a world full of pain and injustice.

2. **"This above all: to thine own self be true,"** (Act 1, Scene 3)

   - Polonius's advice to his son, Laertes, stressing the importance of integrity and self-awareness.

3. **"Something is rotten in the state of Denmark."** (Act 1, Scene 4)

   - Marcellus's comment to Horatio, hinting at the underlying corruption and moral decay in Denmark following King Hamlet's death.

4. **"The lady doth protest too much, methinks."** (Act 3, Scene 2)

   - Queen Gertrude's response to the Player Queen's declarations of love in the play-within-a-play, which ironically mirrors her own situation.

5. **"Frailty, thy name is woman!"** (Act 1, Scene 2)

   ○ Hamlet's harsh criticism of his mother, Gertrude, for her quick remarriage to Claudius, reflecting his disillusionment with women.

6. **"There are more things in heaven and earth, Horatio, Than are dreamt of in your philosophy."** (Act 1, Scene 5)

   ○ Hamlet's remark to Horatio, emphasizing the limitations of human understanding and the existence of supernatural elements.

7. **"Give me that man That is not passion's slave, and I will wear him In my heart's core, ay, in my heart of heart, As I do thee."** (Act 3, Scene 2)

   ○ Hamlet's expression of his admiration for Horatio's stoicism and rationality.

8. **"O, that this too too solid flesh would melt, Thaw and resolve itself into a dew!"** (Act 1, Scene 2)

   ○ Hamlet's expression of his wish to escape his corporeal existence and the burdens of life.

9. **"The play's the thing Wherein I'll catch the conscience of the king."** (Act 2, Scene 2)

   ○ Hamlet's plan to use the performance of "The Murder of Gonzago" to reveal Claudius's guilt in the murder of King Hamlet.

   ○

10. **"Alas, poor Yorick! I knew him, Horatio: a fellow of infinite jest, of most excellent fancy."** (Act 5, Scene 1)

- ○ Hamlet's reflection upon holding the skull of Yorick, the king's jester, contemplating mortality and the inevitable fate that awaits all, regardless of status or humor.

Each of these quotes encapsulates different facets of the play's exploration of themes such as existence, morality, loyalty, and the human condition.